The Overcoming series was initiated by PETER COOPER, Professor of Psychology at the University of Reading and Honorary NHS Consultant Clinical Psychologist. His original book on bulimia nervosa and binge-eating founded the series in 1993 and continues to help many thousands of people in the USA, the UK and Europe. The aim of the series is to help people with a wide range of common problems and disorders to take control of their own recovery program using the latest techniques of cognitive behavioural therapy. Each book, with its specially tailored program, is devised by a practising clinician. Many books in the Overcoming series are now recommended by the UK Department of Health under the Books on Prescription scheme. Self-help (books and other reading materials based on cognitive behavioural therapy principles) is one of the top three treatments for panic disorder, recommended by the National Institute for Health and Clinical Excellence (NICE).

PROFESSOR DERRICK SILOVE is a clinical psychiatrist and Director of the Centre for Population Mental Health Research and the Psychiatry Research and Teaching Unit at the School of Psychiatry, the University of New South Wales. He has worked for many years in the area of anxiety and traumatic stress, his main area of clinical work, research, service development and teaching. ASSOCIATE PROFESSOR VIJAYA MANICAVASAGAR is a Senior Clinical Psychologist and Associate Professor within the Black Dog Institute, School of Psychiatry at the University of New South Wales. As the Director of Psychological Services at the Black Dog Institute she is responsible for developing and implementing a range of education programs for training mental health professionals in the diagnosis and treatment of mood disorders. Vijaya maintains a strong interest in the anxiety disorders and has published widely in this field.

Other titles in the Overcoming series:

3-part self-help courses

Overcoming Anxiety Self-Help Course
Overcoming Bulimia Nervosa and Binge-Eating Self-Help Course
Overcoming Low Self-Esteem Self-Help Course
Overcoming Social Anxiety and Shyness Self-Help Course

Self-help course single-volume books

Overcoming Anger and Irritability
Overcoming Anorexia Nervosa
Overcoming Anxiety
Bulimia Nervosa and Binge-Eating
Overcoming Childhood Trauma
Overcoming Chronic Fatigue
Overcoming Chronic Pain
Overcoming Compulsive Gambling
Overcoming Depression
Overcoming Insomnia and Sleep Problems
Overcoming Low Self-Esteem
Overcoming Mood Swings
Overcoming Obsessive Compulsive Disorder
Overcoming Panic
Overcoming Paranoid and Suspicious Thoughts
Overcoming Problem Drinking
Overcoming Relationship Problems
Overcoming Sexual Problems
Overcoming Social Anxiety and Shyness
Overcoming Traumatic Stress
Overcoming Weight Problems
Overcoming Your Smoking Habit

OVERCOMING PANIC AND AGORAPHOBIA SELF-HELP COURSE

A 3-part programme based on Cognitive Behavioural Techniques

Part One: About Panic Attacks and Agoraphobia

Derrick Silove

and Vijaya Manicavasagar

ROBINSON
London

Constable & Robinson Ltd
3 The Lanchesters
162 Fulham Palace Road
London W6 9ER
www.overcoming.co.uk

First published in the UK by Robinson,
an imprint of Constable & Robinson Ltd 2006

Important Note
This book is not intended as a substitute for medical advice or treatment.
Any person with a condition requiring medical attention should consult
a qualified medical practitioner or suitable therapist.

ISBN-13: 978-1-84529-439-7 (Pack ISBN)
ISBN-10: 1-84529-439-4

ISBN-13: 978-1-84529-549-3 (Part One)
ISBN-10: 1-84529-549-8

ISBN-13: 978-1-84529-550-9 (Part Two)
ISBN-10: 1-84529-550-1

ISBN-13: 978-1-84529-551-6 (Part Three)
ISBN-10: 1-84529-551-X

1 3 5 7 9 10 8 6 4 2

Printed and bound in the EU

Contents

Foreword by Peter Cooper   vii

Introduction   ix

SECTION 1: What are Panic Disorder and Agoraphobia?   1

SECTION 2: How Panic Disorder and Agoraphobia
Affect People's Lives   11

SECTION 3: What Causes Panic and Agoraphobia?   19

SECTION 4: How Can Panic Disorder and Agoraphobia
be Treated?   39

SECTION 5: The Defining Features of Panic and Agoraphobia   51

Extra Charts and Worksheets   57

Thoughts and Reflections   62

Foreword by Peter Cooper

The *Overcoming Panic and Agoraphobia Self-Help Course* is an adaptation of Professor Silove and Associate Professor Manicavasagar's self-help book called *Overcoming Panic*. This book provided a clear account of the nature of panic and its development, and a set of practical strategies for tackling the various components of the problem. These strategies derive from a 'cognitive-behavioural' formulation of panic – as such, they are strategies designed to change the behaviour and thoughts which provoke and maintain panic. The book, first published in 1997, has helped several thousand people in Britain and elsewhere with panic and agoraphobia problems and it continues to prove enormously popular. It is being increasingly widely recommended by clinicians to their patients. In its current new form, as a set of workbooks, it has been updated and reformatted to make it even more accessible and easy to use.

In Part One the authors provide an explanation of the nature of panic disorder and agoraphobia and an account of how they develop and affect people's lives. In Part Two they outline ways of identifying panic triggers, consider the impact of certain lifestyle factors, and specify ways of controlling panic attacks. Finally, in Part Three they explain how to change unhelpful thinking patterns, how to deal with unpleasant physical sensations, and how to overcome agoraphobic tendencies.

Professor Peter Cooper
University of Reading, June 2006

Introduction: How to Use this Workbook

This is a self-help course for dealing with panic and agoraphobia. It has two aims:

1 To help you develop a better understanding of panic and agoraphobia

2 To teach you practical skills to help you manage and overcome your symptoms

Using a self-help approach

A number of techniques are available to control and manage panic attacks. *The Overcoming Panic and Agoraphobia Self-Help Course* will guide you through some of these skills to help yourself. The course is divided into three parts and offers a first step in combating panic attacks and agoraphobia. You can work through the course on your own or with a friend, or you may like to work with the support of your health-care practitioner or therapist.

What does the course involve?

The three workbooks include a number of questionnaires, charts, worksheets and practical exercises for you to work through. Part One helps you to understand anxiety and panic, and Parts Two and Three set out a six-step self-help course to help you systematically overcome these problems. Part One will probably take two to three weeks to complete, while Parts Two and Three may each take three to four weeks to work through.

It is important to take your time and make sure you are happy with each stage before you move on to the next. There is more detailed information about working through the six-step course at the beginning of Part Two.

Will I benefit from the course?

There are broadly four groups of people who should find this course helpful:

1 People who have panic attacks, with or without agoraphobia, and are interested in learning specific skills to combat anxiety and control panic symptoms and agoraphobia.

2 People who have had panic attacks in the past and who want to learn techniques to prevent the symptoms coming back. Getting to know the early symptoms and how to combat them will help you feel confident about preventing relapse.

3 People who are familiar with the basic principles of anxiety management but who have not incorporated these skills into a structured programme. The skills are likely to be less effective if you use them in a haphazard manner or if you don't practise them regularly.

4 Relatives and friends who want to support you by getting a better understanding of panic disorder and agoraphobia. It's sometimes difficult for the people close to you to know how to help or what to suggest. Getting their support can be very useful, as long as they offer appropriate and constructive advice and support.

What does each part cover?

Part One explains:

- What panic disorder and agoraphobia are

- How panic disorder and agoraphobia affect people's lives

- What causes panic and agoraphobia

- How panic disorder and agoraphobia can be treated

- The defining features of panic attacks, panic disorder and agoraphobia

Part Two explains:

- How to use the six-step course

- Step 1: how to recognize when you are anxious and identify panic triggers

- Step 2: how to change lifestyle factors that contribute to panic attacks

- Step 3: how to control panic attacks

Part Three explains:

- Step 4: how to challenge unhelpful thinking styles

- Step 5: how to deal with physical sensations

- Step 6: how to overcome agoraphobia and troubleshoot problem areas

- How to prevent setbacks

How to get the most from the course

Here are some tips to help you get the most from the course:

- These workbooks are practical tools: use the space provided to complete the exercises, and feel free to use the pages to jot down any thoughts or notes, or highlight anything that's particularly useful. This will keep all of your notes in one place, which will be helpful when you come to read back through them later on.

- Keep an open mind and be willing to experiment with new ideas and skills. These workbooks will sometimes ask you to think about painful issues. This may be difficult, but if anxiety, panic and agoraphobia are restricting your life it's worth making the effort to overcome these problems – the rewards will be substantial.

- It's important to commit time to the course to get the most out of it – so set aside up to half an hour each day to complete the practical exercises.

- Try to answer all of the questions and complete all of the exercises, even if you have to come back to some of them later. There may be times when you get stuck and can't think of how to take things forward. If this happens, don't get angry with yourself or give up. Just put the workbook aside and come back to it later, when you're feeling more relaxed.

- You may find it helpful to have the support of a friend – two heads are often better than one. And if both of you are working through the course you may be able to encourage each other to carry on, even when one of you is finding it hard.

- Use the 'Thoughts and Reflections' section at the back of each workbook to write down anything that you find particularly helpful.

- Reread the workbooks. You may get more out of them once you've had a chance to think about some of the ideas and put them into practice.

- The course is designed so that each workbook builds on what has already been covered – for instance, what you learn in Part One will help you when you come to Part Two. While you can dip into the different sections of Part One, it's important to work through the six-step course in Parts Two and Three systematically. Don't progress to the next step until you've practised and mastered the previous one. It doesn't matter how long it takes you to work through the six steps – what's most important is to understand the techniques and practise the skills.

When should you seek further assistance?

Some people with symptoms of panic may need more help and support than these workbooks can provide. If you fall into one of the seven categories described below, it's likely that you'll benefit from the help of a doctor or therapist:

1   People who have any of the rare physical conditions that mimic panic attacks – described in Section 3 of Part One. It's important to consult your doctor if you suspect that you may have one of these conditions.

2   People with severe agoraphobia – especially if it is unrelated to symptoms of panic. These workbooks are for people suffering primarily from panic disorder, who may or may not have some degree of agoraphobia.

3   People with severe depression associated with panic disorder, who might not have the motivation to work through a self-help book on their own. There's a brief guide to managing depression after this introduction.

4   People who lack the confidence to work on their own, or who feel that a self-help course isn't enough. It's important to be fully motivated to follow this course – if you practise the techniques half-heartedly you're unlikely to get good results.

5   People with a strong resistance to making changes in their life.

6   People who have panic attacks and agoraphobia as only one aspect of wider emotional, social or personality problems. For example, if you respond to stress by misusing drugs or alcohol, you may need to seek counselling for substance abuse before (or at the same time as) trying to overcome panic disorder.

7   People with severe mental health issues – for example people who are severely depressed or have psychosis. In these cases it's important to seek the help of a mental health professional.

A Note on Depression

It's quite common for depression and anxiety to go hand in hand. But if you have panic disorder it's unlikely that you'll feel depressed all of the time – it's more usual for these feelings to be fleeting or relatively minor. It might be that you feel depressed for a short while because you've experienced a setback or that you're having to cope with more everyday stress than you've been used to for a while. Some people experience a few days of depressed mood following a panic attack.

As long as you feel positive about life most of the time, it's likely that you'll be able to sustain your energy and motivation to continue learning and practising the techniques to help you overcome panic attacks and agoraphobia. But if you find that you're depressed all or most of the time, and this feeling becomes overwhelming, it's time to get some professional help.

How to deal with minor depression

You can use a self-help approach to combat minor bouts of depression that last a few hours or days. Try these steps:

- Write a list of the stressors that are making you feel depressed, and use the problem-solving technique you learnt in Step 6 to work through any problems.

- Use the techniques in Step 3 to focus your mind on things that you enjoy or which give you pleasure. This is a good approach if you can't easily deal with whatever's making you feel depressed.

- Negative thinking can make you feel depressed. So take another look at Step 4, where you learnt how to identify and challenge negative thinking, and substitute these unhelpful thoughts with more positive and constructive ones.

Dealing with depression

↓

Write down the stressors you face and try to work out step-by-step strategies to deal with them

↓

Do something that helps raise your self-esteem – engage in an activity that's pleasurable and non-stressful

↓

Examine whether your thoughts about yourself, your situation and the future are excessively negative. Challenge these negative thoughts and try to replace them with helpful ones

↓

If your symptoms persist, or if you feel desperate and you're unable to cope, seek professional help

↙   ↘

Regular counselling sessions   Hospitalization
and/or medication

It's important to get some professional help if these self-help techniques don't make you feel better, or you start to feel hopeless or desperate. Don't try to battle it out yourself – there's lots of support available if you ask for help.

Your doctor may suggest an antidepressant medicine and/or regular counselling sessions to help you get through your depression. If you're severely depressed, you may need intensive treatment such as a stay in hospital – being looked after like this can help your recovery and protect you from neglecting or harming yourself and eventually put you back on the road to recovery.

SECTION 1: What are Panic Disorder and Agoraphobia?

This section will help you understand:

- What a normal level of anxiety is

- What a panic attack is, what it feels like to have one, and how you might feel afterwards

- What panic disorder is

- What agoraphobia is

- Why some people develop agoraphobia

- What brings on panic attacks and agoraphobia

For the defining features of panic and agoraphobia see Section 5.

What is a normal level of anxiety?

It is quite usual to feel anxious in stressful situations – in fact it's so common that it's seen as normal. There's even a benefit – feeling mildly anxious actually helps you to perform well in situations that require concentration, efficiency and skill.

Imagine how you would feel in the following situations and put a cross on the line, between 0 (calm and confident) and 10 (extremely anxious):

You're waiting to be called in for a job interview.

0   5   10

You've been asked to give a speech at a friend's wedding, and it's nearly time to stand up and speak.

0   5   10

You've got your driving test today.

0   5   10

You've got to make a train journey which involves a couple of changes where the connections are tight.

0   5   10

You're a manager and you need to reprimand a member of staff.

0   5   10

If most of your crosses lie towards '0', then it's likely that these and other stressful situations make you only mildly anxious. But if your crosses are nearer '10', on the right of the page, your anxiety levels are likely to be high in these and other stressful situations. You may find it disabling if you tend to become severely anxious – your mind might go blank when you open the exam paper for instance, or you may be unable to speak to your audience. People who persistently experience intense feelings of anxiety may have an anxiety disorder.

Anxiety disorders are common and many sufferers try to cope on their own. Some suffer in silence, or use risky methods – drugs and alcohol for instance – to damp down their feelings. Only a portion seek help to treat their anxiety. If you have a panic disorder, using this series of workbooks may help you to understand and work through your feelings, and bring your panic under control.

What is a panic attack?

A panic attack is an episode of sudden and intense anxiety, which often appears out of the blue. It can happen when you least expect it – for instance in a situation where you might not expect to be nervous or frightened, such as getting the bus to work. Panic attacks usually last a few minutes to an hour but the unpleasant after-effects can last for several days.

CASE STUDY: John

'I began having panic attacks when I was about nineteen, during a stressful time at work. I would become breathless and sweaty, my heart would pound, and I had pains in my chest. I became so frightened that I thought I would have a heart attack or die. After that, attacks came out of the blue, and I noticed that I was avoiding certain situations, such as visiting department stores or travelling on buses. I felt that I couldn't talk to anyone about the problem because they would think I was going crazy.'

Panic attacks are frightening, especially if you have no idea that you have an anxiety disorder. Panic produces physical symptoms, which can be so overwhelming that you're sure something far more serious is happening, such as a heart attack. And when you've had a panic attack once in a particular setting, it's likely that you'll want to try to avoid similar situations to stop it happening again.

Panic attacks:

- Involve a sudden burst of anxiety

- Create intense physical symptoms which can affect your whole body

- Cause you to have catastrophic thoughts

- Can last between two minutes and half an hour

- Make you feel frightened and helpless

- Leave you feeling weak and exhausted

- Can occur several times a week, or even daily

What does it feel like to have a panic attack?

CASE STUDY: Christine

'It starts when I suddenly feel like I can't breathe properly. I then start feeling dizzy and sweaty and notice that my heart is racing. Sometimes I become nauseous or feel like I am going to choke. My fingers go numb and I have a tingling sensation in my feet. I feel strange, as if I am not really "there", as if I am detached from reality. I start thinking that I am about to lose control or die. This makes me feel extremely frightened ... Even though the attack only lasts for five or ten minutes, it feels like forever and that I will never get over it.'

Think back over the last few months, and focus on any times when you've felt a sudden burst of severe anxiety. Look at the lists of thoughts and physical symptoms below, and put a tick next to any that you've experienced:

What was going through your mind?

☐ I'm going crazy/insane

☐ I'm going to lose control

☐ I'm going to faint

☐ I'm going to collapse

☐ I'm having a heart attack

☐ I'm having a stroke

☐ I'm going to start screaming and make a fool of myself

How did you feel?

☐ I was short of breath and it was difficult to breathe

☐ I felt like I was choking

☐ My chest felt tight and painful

☐ I felt shaky and weak, and my hands were trembling

☐ I started to sweat more than usual

☐ My hands and feet felt tingly and numb

☐ My heart was pounding, and I felt palpitations in my chest

☐ I felt faint and dizzy – I needed to sit down

☐ I felt 'out of touch' with my body and my surroundings

☐ I felt sick – my stomach was churning and I wanted to run to the toilet

☐ I felt hot and cold, and my face was flushed

☐ I felt like escaping or getting out of the situation quickly

These thoughts and feelings are all common signs of a panic attack – if you've ticked more than a few of the boxes in each section, it's likely that you've experienced a panic attack.

Once your panic subsides, and you're thinking rationally again, you may feel silly for thinking such catastrophic thoughts. But in the moment, the symptoms of panic are frighteningly real. The chances of having a heart attack or a stroke are remote. But once you've had a panic attack, it's difficult to ignore the nagging worry that it will happen again, which can make you feel more anxious in-between attacks.

CASE STUDY: Fay

'Every episode is slightly different. At first I used to feel that I was about to vomit or have diarrhoea. More recently, I have had this severe choking feeling and sharp pain in my chest. I realize now that those feelings of being detached from myself and the environ-ment are part of the same pattern.'

How will you feel after a panic attack?

Once a panic attack is over, most people feel exhausted, dispirited and confused. It's an intensely frightening experience, especially when you don't know why it happened, and this can be very draining. Some people book a check-up with their doctor to find out if they're physically ill. But it's not always easy to talk about what's happened or to seek professional help, especially if you feel ashamed or embarrassed by panicking and losing control.

What is panic disorder?

If you begin to have attack after attack, panic can soon start to interfere with your life. This is known as panic disorder and it affects 2–4 per cent of us at some time in our lives. But even if you've only experienced one or two severe attacks, the anticipation of having another one (anticipatory anxiety) can become so great that this, in itself, leads to panic disorder.

It's difficult not to become preoccupied with the fear of having another panic attack. It can become your biggest concern – when you're out shopping you may worry that any slight stress is going to set things off, so you avoid busy shops. You might even start making excuses to friends to avoid going out and facing stressful situations. The worry about having a panic attack can impact on your life just as much as the attacks themselves, and one of the key elements in recovering from panic disorder and agoraphobia is to overcome anticipatory anxiety. We'll cover some techniques to change negative thinking leading to the 'fear of fear' in Part Three, Section 4 (Step 4 of the self-help course).

What is agoraphobia?

CASE STUDY: Mavis

'After a while I became afraid of going shopping in case I couldn't get back home quickly enough. I felt more and more anxious waiting at the checkout, and on one occasion I had to leave my shopping trolley there and hurry home. After that, I could only go to the shops if someone came with me. My fears extended to other situations so that I began to avoid public transport and even driving in the car. Now I can hardly leave the house.'

Do you avoid certain situations or places because they make you feel very anxious, or because you're worried about having a panic attack? Spend a few minutes thinking about this and then make a list of stressful situations that lead to panic in the space below.

_____

_____

_____

_____

_____

_____

_____

_____

_____

If you've had a panic attack, it may begin to colour the way you see the world – so if you've had an attack in a large department store, you may begin to avoid going shopping altogether. Public transport, crowded places or being in traffic can become off-limits because they remind you that you've had panic attacks in these situations.

Avoiding places to prevent anxiety is called agoraphobia – it's a Greek word that means 'a fear of the market place'. But it's not just about a fear of shopping or public places – simply being home alone can make some people very anxious. Agoraphobia is fairly common – over 7 per cent of women and nearly 3 per cent of men have the disorder at some time in their lives.

Having an easy means of escape from a situation or a place – in case you have a panic attack – takes on real importance if you have agoraphobia, and may be the only thing that makes something tolerable. Or you might find that you can only go somewhere if you've got a close friend with you, to turn to if you start to panic.

The table opposite lists some common situations that people with agoraphobia might avoid, or which can make them anxious. The second column lists the types of behaviour that they might display to try to make these situations more bearable. Use the blank rows at the bottom of the table to write down any situations that make you anxious, and the coping mechanisms you use.

Situation	Coping mechanism
Sitting in a car in traffic	Never driving alone
Going through a tunnel or over a bridge	Avoiding travelling by train
Seeing a play at the theatre	Sitting in an aisle seat, close to the exit
Shopping at a department store or supermarket	Only shopping at stores with street entrances
Taking the lift	Only ever using the stairs
Being at home, alone	Going or staying out, rather than being left alone
Using public transport	Only ever walking, cycling or going by car
Sitting in the waiting room at the doctor's surgery	Phoning to speak to a practice nurse

It's quite common for a fear of a particular situation to grow to include all situations that are similar to the one in which your panic attack first occurred – so if you've had a panic attack in one restaurant, you may start to avoid all restaurants. This avoidance behaviour can escalate, and you can quickly find that your set of 'rules' for what you will and won't do severely restricts the way you live your life. For some people this may mean that they never leave home. These avoidance techniques may be so 'successful' that the panic attacks stop – but the avoidance becomes a habit, and then a way of life.

There's a complex relationship between panic disorder and agoraphobia. Quite a lot of people with panic disorder develop agoraphobia; but not everyone does – this is called 'pure' panic disorder. And agoraphobia is not necessarily linked to panic disorder – it can occur on its own, or as part of another disorder, such as depression. Even if you've stopped having panic attacks, you may still have agoraphobia.

Why do some people develop agoraphobia?

It's still not clear why some people with panic disorder develop agoraphobia, but it's likely that two mechanisms come into play.

- **A 'fear of fear'** If you repeatedly have a panic attack in a particular situation, it's only natural that you'll develop a fear that the same thing will happen every time you approach that situation, or do something similar. So your mind uses your past experience as 'solid evidence' of what could happen, and warns you off places or situations where you experienced panic. This 'fear of fear' is usually influenced by worrisome thoughts, which drive your anxiety and avoidance behaviours.

- **Automatic 'conditioning'** Pavlov's dog was conditioned to salivate every time a bell was rung, and we can be 'conditioned' in the same way. If you always feel anxious when you approach a certain situation – say getting on a bus – then you'll automatically condition yourself to feel anxious at the prospect of a bus journey. Without knowing it, you begin to associate panic with situations where it has occurred in the past, even if those places are not genuinely dangerous. Some of us are more susceptible and may 'condition' more easily than others – just having a few panic attacks in a department store may mean you 'learn' to avoid shopping there.

People cope in different ways with their worries and this may influence the likelihood of developing agoraphobia. For instance, these four factors can increase the risk:

- Lacking confidence – you're more likely to want to avoid stress and tend to withdraw.

- A strong fear of separation ('separation anxiety') – you may tend to cling to others for security, or only go out in the company of a trusted friend.

- Having panic disorder – 60 per cent of people with panic disorder develop agoraphobia.

- Being a woman – more women than men with panic disorder develop agoraphobia. This may be related to cultural expectations: men are expected (and therefore expect themselves) to 'soldier on' and to fight anxiety, although often with the 'help' of alcohol.

What brings on panic attacks and agoraphobia?

If you think about it, it's likely that you'll be able to recall several stressful incidents that occurred in the weeks or months before you started to have panic attacks. Some of these 'stressors' may have continued or even worsened after the attacks began. These are some common examples of stressors:

- Arguments with your spouse or partner

- The death of a family member or close friend

- Being ill

- Having problems at work

Everyone experiences these types of stress, but not everyone goes on to develop panic attacks. The trigger usually involves a particularly threatening combination of factors for that person, such as being physically and/or psychologically vulnerable, as well as experiencing life stress. And being stressed can play a part in causing panic attacks to continue. The next section looks at how a range of different factors can cause a 'vicious cycle of panic' to develop.

Summary

- Nearly everyone feels anxious in situations such as job interviews, but this can actually make you perform better. If stressful situations cause you severe, disabling anxiety, and this happens frequently, you may have an anxiety disorder.

- A panic attack is an episode of sudden and intense anxiety, which often appears out of the blue and in situations that you wouldn't normally think would cause such a severe reaction. You might tremble, become sweaty and have a pounding heart – which is likely to make you think you're seriously ill.

- Panic attacks are frightening and can leave you drained and confused. Having repeated attacks leads to panic disorder – the anticipation of another attack can have just as much impact on your life as the attacks themselves.

- Agoraphobia is when you avoid certain places or situations because they make you feel anxious, or because you fear you might have a panic attack. People with agoraphobia need to have an easy escape route and tend to avoid situations such as sitting in traffic or being in large crowds; it can also include a fear of being home alone.

- Two main mechanisms come into play when people develop agoraphobia. A 'fear of fear' means you'll avoid places where you've experienced panic in the past. And 'automatic conditioning' is where you begin to associate a situation or place with feelings of panic, even if there is no genuine danger.

- Stressful life events, as well as a combination of other physical and psychological factors, can trigger panic attacks.

SECTION 2: How Panic Disorder and Agoraphobia Affect People's Lives

This section will help you understand:

- How panic disorder and agoraphobia can lead to depression
- What depression is
- How panic disorder and agoraphobia can impact on your social life

How panic disorder and agoraphobia can lead to depression

CASE STUDY: Patricia

'My life revolves around the fear of having another panic attack. I can't concentrate on my work, which has suffered greatly. My problem has caused family rows. My family think that I should just pull myself together and stop worrying. I have lost my self-confidence and self-respect. I don't like to socialize any more in case I embarrass myself or I'm forced to leave in a hurry because of a panic attack.'

Having panic attacks and/or agoraphobia – especially if you avoid certain situations – can interfere with all aspects of your life, including your:

- Work
- Studies
- Relationships with your family, spouse or partner
- Social life.

If the fear of having another panic attack is always at the back of your mind, you'll probably feel apprehensive, tense and fearful. When you feel like this you'll begin to approach each day with caution, and this can make you unadventurous and constrained. So it's not surprising that people with panic disorder and agoraphobia often become depressed.

What is depression?

CASE STUDY: Geoffrey

'Sometimes I would start to cry and cry ... I felt so hopeless and useless. Other people around me seemed to be able to run their own lives ... but for me panic attacks were controlling my life. Why couldn't I just snap out of it and be OK? I started feeling more and more depressed and self-critical as I realized that I couldn't control the panic attacks. I lost my self-confidence, I stopped wanting to socialize, and my friends seemed to withdraw from me. Life became so difficult that the thought crossed my mind that it was not worth going on.'

Between 30 and 70 per cent of people with panic disorder develop depression at some point, on top of their symptoms of anxiety. Depressive symptoms can last for hours or days at a time, and periods of depression can stretch on for weeks or even months. Depressed mood can vary in severity, from mild to severe:

Mild depression		Severe depression
Feeling sad and tearful	Feelings of hopelessness, worthlessness and failure	Suicidal thoughts

If you're depressed, you might not feel able to work or socialize – not only because you're frightened of having a panic attack, but also because of the feelings that go hand-in-hand with being severely demoralized, such as:

● Having low self-esteem

● Losing interest in doing things, such as seeing friends

● Feeling unable to enjoy yourself

It's common to feel a sense of shame if you're unable to control your anxiety, which only serves to make things worse. Shame makes us secretive about anxiety, so you might find yourself saying 'no' to what could be an enjoyable night out with friends because you'd rather stay in than reveal your problems. This can lead to a vicious cycle of avoiding enjoyable activities:

Avoiding social situations

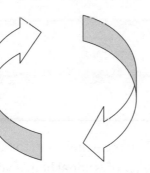

You feel shame about
your anxiety

Increasing feelings of isolation

You become more self-critical
and withdrawn

Depression worsens, leading
to further loss of motivation

Feelings of hopelessness

If you have agoraphobia you may find that you'll go to great lengths to gain some control over your panic and anxiety by restricting the way you live – and this in itself can lead to depression. When you feel depressed, all of the symptoms of anxiety, avoidance and depression may interact, which can be even more disabling and upsetting. It's really important to recognize these vicious cycles and attempt to break them as part of the recovery process.

If you have panic attacks you might feel quite desperate at times because it can seem that there's no way out – no way to improve your situation. You might start to look for ways to comfort yourself or blot out the symptoms.

Think about how you try to cope with your anxiety and depression, and tick any types of behaviour in the list below that you find yourself doing. There's space on the next page to write down any thoughts you may experience when you feel anxious or depressed:

- [ ] Overeating
- [ ] Drinking excessively
- [ ] Smoking
- [ ] Overspending
- [ ] Using recreational drugs
- [ ] Overusing prescribed medicines

_____

_____

_____

_____

_____

Although this series of workbooks can help you to take steps to overcome your panic disorder, it's important to seek professional help if you're consistently depressed and particularly if you have any ideas about self-harm, or you're having suicidal thoughts.

Once most people with panic disorder and agoraphobia are able to bring their anxiety symptoms under control, their depressed mood tends to lift. In a few cases it may linger after you've started to feel less anxious, so if you find that you're still depressed it's important to seek specialist professional help. If you're not sure which is the main problem – depression or anxiety – it's best to talk to your doctor.

How panic disorder and agoraphobia can impact on your social life

CASE STUDY: Joanne

'My anxiety problem has taken over my whole life. Even though I have a close family, I can't talk to any of them about it because they don't understand what I am going through. My problem has created a wall between me and my husband. Also, I become terribly embarrassed with my friends when I start developing panic symptoms. I can't face seeing people.'

Another difficulty of coping with panic attacks is the profound effect they can have on your family and your social life – especially because your attacks may involve being out of the house among other people. And it can be difficult to decide whether or not to tell people what you're going through, for fear of what they might say or how they'll react.

If you don't tell your friends and family they can become frustrated and offended when you repeatedly turn down their invitations. And sometimes, sharing your problem can be met with unhelpful or negative comments and advice, or people might not take you seriously.

Have you ever talked to someone close to you about your anxiety? What did they say, and how did this make you feel? Spend a few minutes writing down your thoughts in the space below.

_____

_____

_____

_____

_____

_____

_____

_____

Superficial advice from the people close to you such as 'pull yourself together' or 'be strong' can seem insensitive. But it's important to remember that most people don't know very much about panic attacks and agoraphobia, and they may not understand how difficult it is to deal with these problems. Most people think that because everyone feels anxious from time to time, it's easy to cope with these feelings by using willpower. Being severely anxious can also disturb intimate relationships, and a vicious circle of misunderstanding can set in:

You're anxious, which makes you irritable, preoccupied, withdrawn or in need of repeated reassurance

You depend heavily on your spouse or partner for reassurance or to do everyday chores such as shopping, banking or collecting the children from school

Your spouse or partner feels baffled, frustrated and helpless

You feel that your spouse or partner doesn't understand your problem

It's likely that your social and personal relationships will be transformed once you've learnt how to master your anxiety and recover from the acute symptoms. You'll begin to feel much happier within your family and your social networks, and your relationship with your partner will be much less strained – a welcome relief for both of you.

You may find that your anxiety and recovery have affected the dynamics within your family – their lifestyles and the way you interact together may reflect the gradual adaptations to the restrictions you'd placed on your own life. So it can take time for things to readjust – especially for the rest of your family to get used to the less-anxious person you're becoming. You're likely to be more active, assertive and independent than they are used to, and this can make everyone feel tense and uncertain for a while. If you find that you're all having trouble getting used to the new way of living together, it can be a good idea for the family as a whole to see a therapist or a counsellor.

Summary

- Panic disorder and agoraphobia can have a serious impact on several aspects of your life. The way you feel can inhibit the way you live your life – being cautious, unadventurous and restrained can lead to depression.

- Between 30 and 70 per cent of people with panic disorder develop depression at some point. Being depressed can lead to a vicious cycle of avoiding enjoyable activities such as going out with friends. You might also feel shame about your anxiety – wanting to hide away and avoid talking about your problems to your close friends and family.

- Your depression and anxiety can impact on the people around you – they may not understand what's going on and offer insensitive advice. They can also feel baffled, frustrated and helpless – this can turn into a vicious cycle of misunderstanding.

- If you're severely depressed it's important to seek professional help – especially if you are at risk of self-harming or having suicidal thoughts.

- As you recover from anxiety and panic disorder you may find that your family has trouble adjusting to the new you – if this becomes a problem it's best for the family as a whole to seek professional help and advice.

SECTION 3: What Causes Panic and Agoraphobia?

This section will help you understand:

- How panic develops

- How your childhood and the effects of later life can make you vulnerable to panic

- Your body's anxiety mechanism

- When it's not panic – illnesses that produce similar symptoms

- What sets off a panic attack

- What perpetuates the vicious cycle of panic

How panic develops

A variety of factors act together to cause panic attacks and panic disorder. It's different for everyone, but it's useful to think of these things as a chain of factors, which builds up progressively to produce panic.

You can broadly group these factors into three types:

- Your vulnerability – your physical make-up, character and life experiences

- The immediate stressors or triggers that bring on a sudden panic attack

- Influences or perpetuating factors that keep the process going, and often lead to a vicious cycle, which makes panic attacks more severe or frequent

What makes you vulnerable?

Some people are more vulnerable than others to developing panic attacks and agoraphobia. A lot is unknown but three types of factors seem to be important in determining your risk:

- Physical

- Psychological

- Social

As you read through the following parts of this section, think about your childhood, your family, your adult life, your experiences and your memories. Jot down anything that strikes you as meaningful or significant on one of the blank 'Thoughts and Reflections' pages at the back of this book.

Risk factors when you are growing up

CASE STUDY: Paul

'When I was young I used to worry about getting breathless. I suffered from asthma at an early age and my mother used to worry that any breathlessness meant that I was about to have an asthma attack. My mum also suffered from panic attacks and she used to get very anxious whenever I came back home exhausted from playing football or riding my bike with my friends. As I got older, I started to worry that I'd also start to have panic attacks when I became breathless. Doing things that got me out of breath started to make me feel anxious, so I stopped playing football and tried not to over-exert myself. Now I feel anxious all the time, and I'm really unfit.

Panic disorder sometimes runs in families. When this happens it can be inherited partly through your genes, shaped by the nature of the relationships between the members of your family, or a mixture of the two. For instance, identical twins may have a similar tendency to worry or be nervy (they have similar levels of 'trait anxiety'), which suggests an inherited tendency to develop symptoms such as panic.

Your family environment and your childhood experiences are also important. Some adults with agoraphobia recall their family environments as being cold and unsupportive. Sometimes, seeing a parent acting in a fearful way sets up a habit in the child. The relationships between children and their parents are always complex, and it's important not to blame each other for creating anxiety. If your parents were overprotective, for example, it's difficult to be sure whether this caused you to feel insecure. Some anxious children demand more, and are less satisfied with the attention they receive from their parents.

Being exposed to shocking events early on in life, such as abuse and trauma, can increase the risk of panic disorder as children grow up. These experiences make people vulnerable to a wide range of emotional difficulties as adults, and some events can be particularly significant. For example, if you experienced something as a child that made it difficult to breathe, such as near-drowning, suffocation, or a severe asthma attack, your nervous system may now be more sensitive to the chemical changes that occur in your blood when your breathing rate changes. If you've had such an experience, hyperventilating (overbreathing) can make you more likely to develop a full-blown panic attack.

Thinking back to your childhood, do you find any of the following statements familiar? Write down anything that comes to mind in each of the spaces below:

I was seldom given any reassurance or support.

_____

_____

My parents were never openly affectionate.

_____

_____

Nobody really encouraged me to develop my confidence.

_____

_____

There was a major disruption in my family.

_____

_____

I experienced a severe shock or trauma.

_____

_____

One of my parents often acted afraid or anxious when they were going out.

_____

_____

Risk factors as an adult

Psychological factors

CASE STUDY: Walter

'Why can't I control myself? Every time I leave the house I feel so anxious – even getting on the bus is more than I can cope with. That's the third time I've had a panic attack and my boss is starting to notice that I'm often late for work. Perhaps I should stop going out altogether. That way I can make sure that I won't have any more of these awful attacks. I'm sure that something terrible is going to happen during one of them – the tightness in my chest must mean there's something wrong with me, even though my doctor has told me that I'm completely healthy. Surely it's safer to stay at home? My life seems to be completely out of control.'

People who are prone to having panic attacks often think in a particular way. For instance, if you experienced a sudden pain or tightness in your chest, what would be your first thought? Circle one of the statements below:

- 'I'm about to have a heart attack'

or

- 'It's probably just a bit of indigestion'

If you circled the first statement, you may be someone who interprets things in a negative or 'catastrophic' way – such as jumping to the conclusion that a brief chest pain means you're having a heart attack. Most people are able to counter unrealistic fears with more positive, reassuring thoughts. If you have trouble doing this you might also tend to:

- Believe that you can't control your life or the world around you

- Slip quickly into thinking that problems are too great to tackle, and beyond your capacity to solve

- Become worried and stressed when you encounter real-life problems

If you're prone to catastrophic thinking, write down three recent examples where you've interpreted something negatively, but which hasn't actually turned out as badly as you feared. First write down what happened, your interpretation of what happened, and then what you realized actually happened, afterwards.

Example 1

_____

_____

_____

Example 2

_____

_____

_____

Example 3

_____

_____

_____

A negative thinking style can grow out of what you learnt or from the things you experienced as a child. When you're a child, negative events often seem uncontrollable at the time. Adults can either reassure you or increase your fears. These experiences can undermine your self-esteem and lead to the feeling that life is worryingly unpredictable and that problems are impossible to solve.

Negative thinking can affect the way you deal with stress. Everyone has different ways of coping with stress or stressful situations, and some people cope better than others. You're likely to have learnt your own set of coping skills from the people around you when you were growing up. These skills become a habit if you use them again and again, but some methods or styles are more helpful than others.

Do you have any of these coping styles? Tick any that sound familiar:

☐ I give up or quickly become frustrated when I face obstacles

☐ I avoid situations that I anticipate may make me feel uncomfortable

☐ I become tense and irritable if I can't get my own way immediately

☐ I often depend on others for help

☐ I take excessive amounts of alcohol or drugs to dampen unpleasant feelings

These are negative coping styles and, if you often feel anxious, these styles can actually make the symptoms worse. But breaking old coping habits and learning new, more helpful ones can be a challenge and takes a bit of practice. You'll find out how to start making these changes in Part Two, Section 4.

Social factors

CASE STUDY: Yvonne

'I've been working day and night for the exams and have had little time to go out with Sam. It's hard to know why things are so cold between us. Is it because I'm so busy or are the attacks I'm having making me more irritable? He seems confused about our relationship but I am scared to tell him about the attacks in case he thinks I am crazy or weak. At the same time, I need his support even more now that my confidence is so low.'

A wide range of people can develop panic attacks and panic disorder, although women are more susceptible than men. It's not clear why this is, but possible reasons include:

- The role of women in modern society

- Genetic or hormonal factors

- The stressors associated with childrearing

- Being pulled in different directions – being both a homebuilder and a breadwinner

Difficulties in relationships can trigger or perpetuate panic disorder but this is a complex area – some people who develop panic attacks are single. So it's not always easy to pin down whether the stress within the family or relationship is a cause or a result of one member having panic disorder.

For example, if one partner is domineering, they may behave like this to compensate for their partner's insecurity. Or it may be that the person in the relationship with panic disorder begins to feel more insecure and dependent as a result of their partner's domineering character, and over time becomes more anxious. Both of these things may even be happening at the same time. Either way, it's important to assess and address relationship factors as part of your recovery from panic disorder.

Physical reactions

CASE STUDY: Frank

*'When I went shopping today I had those spasms in my chest again – I felt that I could-
n't breathe, that my chest was in a vice, and that pins were being stuck into my heart. It's
nothing new – this has been happening for months now. I keep going back to the hospital, but they just say they can find "nothing wrong". How can I have chest pains this
severe and be physically fit? It doesn't make sense – the symptoms are so real, I'm sure
they are missing something serious like a heart condition – I'm really scared that I'm
going to have a heart attack when I'm out shopping one day, and die.'*

If you've experienced a panic attack you've probably wondered whether your symptoms are real or just a result of your 'imagination'. To understand why your body
reacts in the way it does, it's helpful to look at what happens after any sort of shock
or stress: the extreme fear it causes is called a 'stress response'. Think how you would
react if a car suddenly turned a corner at high speed and narrowly missed you as you
crossed the street; or if someone unexpectedly slammed a door behind you. You
might:

- Suddenly become very alert and vigilant

- Feel your skin crawling and break into a sweat

- Have a pounding heart

- Feel shaky

- Jump up, shout or get angry

Your body's response to a shock or threat is called the 'fight or flight' response, and
it helps you to take defensive action when you feel threatened. This response is
instantaneous and automatic – it happens without any conscious prompting from the
thinking centres in your brain.

Other centres in your brain coordinate your hormonal and involuntary (or 'autonomic') nervous system, which in turn controls the muscles of your internal organs
and glands. The involuntary nervous system is activated as soon as your brain
receives a threatening message from the outside world. When those nerves send out
an alarm signal, it sets off a chain reaction as shown in the diagram on the next page.

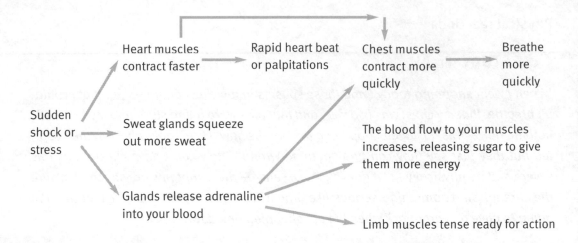

This fear reaction makes you alert to the environment and could save your life in an emergency. The physical sensations you experience – such as a racing heart – are caused by actual physiological changes, and usually pass after the threat has disappeared. But the fine-tuning of the 'fight or flight' response in people with panic disorder works slightly differently:

- The response might be activated inappropriately, when there is no direct threat

- The 'trigger' threshold may be lower

- The control mechanism for bringing the fight or flight response to an end may be less efficient

- Other unknown factors keep it going

If you suffer from panic disorder, a number of factors can mean your body operates closer and closer to the trigger threshold. For instance, your temperament – say you have a tendency to worry – plus continuing stress over a period of time adds up to an increase in the tension in your body. When this happens even minor events can set off the fight or flight response, leading to panic.

If you're the type of person who interprets things in a catastrophic way, you'll keep sending 'false alarms' to the centre that triggers the fight or flight reaction. If your body triggers this response inappropriately – say when a situation is stressful, but not really dangerous – you can experience the symptoms of a panic attack. If you then become frightened by the physical symptoms ('my heart's racing – am I having a heart attack?') it can become a vicious circle with repeated false alarms triggering panic. It's important to remember that the fight or flight response itself is a normal and useful mechanism and, if you're otherwise healthy, the physical symptoms of panic won't directly damage your health.

Fight or flight response

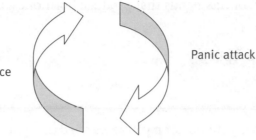

Stressful experience

Panic attack

Frightened by panic symptoms

Anxiety mechanisms in the nervous system

Chemicals called 'neurotransmitters' pass messages between nerves in the brain for fear, alarm and anxiety. It's not clear whether these 'messenger' systems are different in the brains of people with anxiety, but many of the medicines that help anxiety (see Part One, Section 4) alter the actions of these neurotransmitters, or the way the nerve endings respond to these messengers.

Any differences are very subtle and probably relate to the fine balance of certain chemicals and their actions in particular brain pathways. Ordinary tests such as X-rays or brain scans cannot detect these fine-tuned abnormalities in people with panic disorder. If your doctor does detect anything, it's likely that the problem isn't a primary panic disorder, but one of the relatively uncommon physical illnesses that sometimes can mimic panic.

Physical illnesses that can cause panic-like symptoms

Some physical illnesses can mimic panic disorder, but this is uncommon. Usually, there will be other symptoms that help your doctor diagnose a physical disorder. Occasionally, anxiety-like symptoms will be the first sign of such an underlying illness.

Some conditions that may cause panic-like symptoms include:

- Excessive use of or withdrawal from caffeine, drugs or alcohol

- Irregular heart rhythms, and occasionally, disease of the heart blood vessels

- Disorders that affect your breathing

- Excessive use of certain medications, e.g. for asthma

- Rare disorders of the glands that produce hormones and other chemicals in the blood

- Certain types of epilepsy

- Rare brain disorders

It's important to see your doctor if you're worried that you may have a serious illness. It's likely that any tests will show that you're physically healthy, which means your symptoms are due to anxiety. Often the doctor will not think that tests are necessary. If you do have a rare physical cause, it's very likely that the appropriate treatment will also reduce your anxiety-like symptoms. Some people have a physical illness such as asthma or heart disease, as well as panic disorder and they will need treatment for both conditions.

Although it's unusual for typical panic symptoms to be caused entirely by a physical illness, attacks can be so dramatic that it's difficult to believe you're otherwise healthy. It's tempting to visit several doctors or insist on repeated tests and complicated investigations. This can be stressful in itself, and reinforce your fear that there 'must be something wrong'. There is a risk that you may interpret statements like *"we cannot find anything wrong"* as meaning that your doctor has missed something. This is very rare! Try to remind yourself that one of the common symptoms of panic disorder is an uncontrollable worry that you have physical illness. So if your doctor rules this out, focus on managing your anxiety symptoms rather than on having more tests.

What sets off a panic attack?

Hyperventilation and panic symptoms

Hyperventilation (overbreathing) is a common trigger for panic symptoms if you're susceptible to them. If you have panic attacks, you may notice that your breathing becomes shallow and the rate increases while you're having the attack.

It's easy to mistake two common signs of anxiety – yawning and sighing – for boredom and sadness, so you may not even be aware that you're chronically hyperventilating. If you notice that you have episodes where your breathing alters in any of the following ways, you may be hyperventilating:

- Feeling like you are not getting enough air

- Shallow, frequent breathing
- Gasping
- Sighing
- Yawning
- Panting

If you find that you're sighing and yawning through the day, you may be chronically overbreathing and putting yourself at risk of provoking panic symptoms and panic attacks. Hyperventilation upsets the normal balance of oxygen and carbon dioxide in your blood. As a result, less oxygen reaches your brain and you feel unsteady, dizzy, 'spaced out' and weak – the typical symptoms of panic.

Over the next few days, try to become more aware of your breathing. A normal rate of breathing is usually between eight and 10 breaths per minute. Is your breathing much faster than this? Are you breathing from your abdomen (deeply) or from your chest (shallow breathing)? You could also ask your partner, family and close friends to give you feedback on whether you repeatedly yawn or sigh. Note down any unusual types of breathing in the spaces below (there is additional space, should you need it, at the back of this workbook):

Day 1

_____

_____

_____

Day 2

_____

_____

_____

Day 3

_____

_____

_____

If you become stressed you're more likely to hyperventilate and, in chronic over-breathers, this can trigger a panic attack. Once the attack starts you'll breathe more rapidly, and the 'hyperventilation–panic' vicious cycle begins. And if you're prone to misinterpreting situations by catastrophic thinking, the physical symptoms of hyperventilation can make you more anxious and increase the feeling of panic.

Hyperventilation (overbreathing)

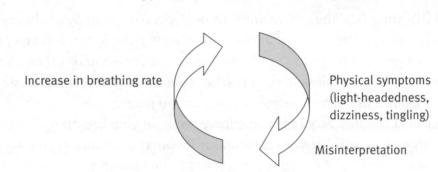

Increase in breathing rate

Physical symptoms
(light-headedness,
dizziness, tingling)

Misinterpretation

Panic symptoms/panic attacks

Misusing alcohol, drugs and medicines

CASE STUDY: Bill

'I found that if I had a few beers before going out, then I was less likely to have the attacks. Over time, I needed to drink more to control the attacks. I found that I woke up shaky in the morning and I needed to have a drink immediately to calm down. I then lost track whether I was still having panic attacks or just needed another drink.'

What do you do to comfort yourself when you're feeling anxious? If you reach for alcohol, drugs such as marijuana, cocaine, amphetamines and other stimulants, or a strong cup of tea or coffee, you may be making things worse. Misusing these things is one of the most important physical factors contributing to anxiety in people with panic disorder. You may think that they'll give you some comfort, but in reality they will provoke and stimulate your nervous system. And using them excessively can lower your panic threshold and increase the risk of having a panic attack.

If you have panic attacks it can be very tempting to use alcohol and sedative drugs (such as benzodiazepines) to try to dampen symptoms of panic, or to give you the courage to go out, for instance. But the positive effect is only short-lived; in the long run your anxiety will become worse. With time, you may begin to need to use more alcohol to control your anxiety, so you'll be more likely to experience withdrawal symptoms. Sedative drugs can have the same effect. These withdrawal effects (such as the 'shakes') are very similar to symptoms of panic, so that the underlying anxiety disorder becomes even more complicated.

As with many of the other contributory factors, the relationship between alcohol or drug use and panic disorder is complex. If you find that you're drinking or using drugs, and you have symptoms of anxiety, ask yourself these questions to get a better understanding of what's going on:

- Which came first? The anxiety or the heavy drinking/drug use?

- Are you increasing your use of drugs or drinking more?

- Is there a relationship between the time since you began using alcohol or drugs and getting shaky?

- Have other people commented on your use of alcohol or drugs?

Think back to when you first became aware of your anxiety symptoms and write down any thoughts below.

_____

_____

_____

_____

_____

_____

Even if alcohol or drug use is the secondary problem, it can cause dependence as well as leading to physical illness and psychological problems, including anxiety. If, on the other hand, your panic symptoms are secondary, bringing your drinking or drug use under control will lessen your anxiety symptoms. Even if the anxiety is primary, the alcohol or drug problem may have become entrenched – if this is the case you'll need to seek treatment for this problem in its own right. It is rarely possible to overcome panic disorder if you continue to abuse alcohol or drugs.

What keeps the vicious cycle going?

Many people have one or two panic attacks in their lives when they are under extreme stress. The experience is very unpleasant, but it is soon forgotten. But for some people, a vicious cycle starts, which causes panic attacks to recur like a chain reaction. The factors that may cause this reaction can be divided into three categories: psychological, social and physical.

Psychological factors

'Fear of fear' and 'fear of illness' can greatly increase the chances of one panic attack leading to another. In some ways, sufferers and their nervous systems are tricking each other. Consider the chain of events in this example where Karen, who is vulnerable to panic, has her first ever panic attack at the supermarket.

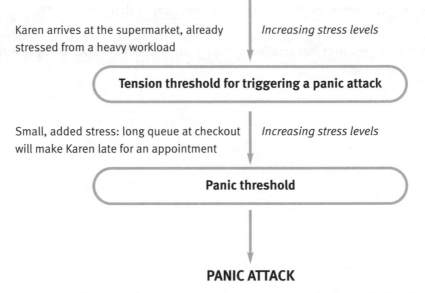

Karen arrives at the supermarket, already stressed from a heavy workload — *Increasing stress levels*

Tension threshold for triggering a panic attack

Small, added stress: long queue at checkout will make Karen late for an appointment — *Increasing stress levels*

Panic threshold

PANIC ATTACK

fight or flight response causes palpitations, sweating, tingling in the hands and feet

Karen's autonomic nervous system is 'fooled' into a state of emergency. Once it is triggered, the full fight or flight response occurs, with Karen's autonomic nervous system 'assuming' that if her tension level is so high, the situation must be dangerous. Because the actual final stress – the long supermarket queue – is only minor, Karen is not consciously aware of any immediate danger and is bewildered by the powerful impulse to 'fight' or 'run away'.

It's understandable and easy to interpret these weird feelings as signs of going mad or losing control. The physical sensations may be linked to the environment because our learning mechanisms are heightened when we're in a state of fear and arousal. Karen may think that these feelings must be symptoms of some serious physical or mental illness. It's no surprise that once the early attacks have subsided, people are left with strong lingering fears that they are ill, about to die or experiencing early signs of mental illness. They may instinctively avoid places where panic tends to occur.

Background factors keep these fears alive and even make them worse. If you're prone to catastrophic thinking, for example, then the fears of imminent death or loss of control will be magnified. And every physical sensation could be a sign that the 'illness' is coming back or getting worse. The situation is made worse by the powerful conditioning effects of having a fight or flight response in a particular situation. To protect you from future 'danger', your nervous system:

'Remembers' what the situation was in which the emergency reaction occurred.
'Warns' you by producing early anxiety symptoms every time you approach that or a similar situation.

Sets up a vicious cycle of fear, avoidance and agoraphobia

Think about your first panic attack and use the space below to write down anything you remember about the chain of events leading up to it. What was causing the underlying stress? What may have triggered the attack? What did you think during and after the attack – did you worry that you were ill? Did you worry about not being able to escape to a place of 'safety'?

_____

_____

_____

_____

_____

Some ways of 'coping' with the situation only make it worse by increasing the pressure and anxiety. This might happen when you:

- Become more pressured in your activities under stress and then manage your time poorly.

- Have a strong need for approval, and find it difficult to say 'no' for fear of rejection. You may accept too many tasks to compensate for the difficulties caused by fear and panic attacks, and try to meet too many demands.

- Avoid 'risky' situations or give up and retreat once you have had your first few panic attacks. You withdraw into yourself and become despondent, and lose your self-esteem and confidence.

- Are so determined to overcome the problem that you force yourself repeatedly into difficult situations without using appropriate techniques to overcome your anxiety.

- Become fearful of seeking help, going mad, or being seen by others as weak or silly.

What are your coping mechanisms? Think about what you do, and the effects, and complete the table below (there are extra tables at the back of this workbook):

Coping mechanism	Effects

Social factors

The social crises that lead to a build-up of tension before the onset of panic disorder may continue and even increase after the attacks begin. The internal stress of worrying about having another panic attack adds to the external stress at work or at home, which leads to a mounting spiral of tension and makes it much more likely that you'll have more panic attacks.

Some people may give up their social, leisure and sporting activities to cope with immediate problems at work – instead of relaxing and going out socially they bring work home to try to 'get on top' of the pressure. Without realizing it, this increases the pressure they're under and makes it more likely that they'll have further panic attacks. Many people become irritable and withdrawn because they feel that the people around them don't understand their anxieties and fears. It's a vicious cycle again, and it soon becomes difficult to see clearly whether the stress is coming from 'outside' or 'inside'.

Have you given up any leisure and social activities or changed your behaviour since you started having panic attacks? Make a list below:

_____

_____

_____

_____

_____

Physical factors

A number of physical factors can bring on and perpetuate panic, and some illnesses cause similar symptoms. Bouts of the flu can mimic anxiety and intensify panic symptoms, although it is relatively rare for a serious physical illness to mimic panic disorder. Look at the checklist below and tick anything that applies to you.

☐ I'm always sighing and yawning

☐ I find it difficult to get to sleep at night

☐ I don't have the time to take regular exercise

☐ I always seem to have a cold

☐ I never wake refreshed

☐ I drink alcohol on most days

☐ I can't function without a strong cup of tea or coffee in the morning

☐ I often skip meals

☐ My heavy workload means I'm often late for meetings – I'm always running to get somewhere.

Most of the physical factors that can lead to panic disorder may also keep it going – if you've ticked three or more of the statements above, you may be adding to the problem. Poor general health, loss of fitness and not getting enough sleep – often provoked by the stress of having panic attacks – only make the situation worse. And if you've got a pressured lifestyle you may overexert yourself by trying to keep on track, and this can also make things worse – running up stairs to get to your office early can produce panic-like sensations such as sweating, a pounding heart and heavy breathing.

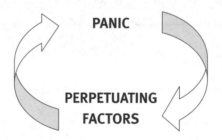

PANIC

PERPETUATING
FACTORS

Psychological factors	Social factors	Physical factors
Ongoing stress	Chronic stress	Hyperventilation
Poor coping with stress	Pressured lifestyle	Poor sleep
Fear of illness	Poor communication	Overexertion
	Little understanding of problems by family and friends	Little or no exercise
Fear of further panic attacks	Family tension	Poor general health
Negative thinking: • catastrophic thinking • loss of sense of control • loss of self-esteem and confidence	Reduction in leisure time	Alcohol
	Social isolation	Drugs

Summary

- A chain of factors builds up progressively to produce panic: you may already be vulnerable, new triggers can bring on a panic attack, and perpetuating factors keep the process going.

- Being vulnerable to panic can be the result of your childhood experiences combined with psychological, social and physical factors later on in life. Negative thinking and catastrophic interpretation can increase the risk of panic attacks.

- The fight or flight response, which causes physical sensations such as a racing heart, heavy breathing, sweating and feeling shaky, is a normal mechanism and can save you from danger. But when it is set off inappropriately, by minor events, it can lead to panic.

- Hyperventilation (overbreathing) is a common trigger for panic symptoms – try to notice whether you yawn or sigh excessively, and practise breathing more evenly.

- Some physical illnesses can mimic the symptoms of panic – always see your doctor if you're worried there's something wrong, but accept the diagnosis of anxiety if it is made.

- Look after your health, take regular exercise, eat a healthy diet and seek help if you find you're coming to depend on drugs or alcohol to deal with feelings of anxiety and panic. Over-reliance on alcohol and drugs can make you feel more anxious and increase the risk of panic attacks.

SECTION 4: How Can Panic Disorder and Agoraphobia be Treated?

This section will help you understand:

- The research that has been done into treating panic disorder and agoraphobia

- The medications available

- The psychological treatments used for panic disorder and agoraphobia

- How medications and psychological treatments can be used together

- Whether treatment will help you

Types of research

There have been impressive advances in recent decades in the way panic disorder is treated. The good news is that with guided practice, most people with panic disorder should make a full recovery. This is the general consensus, going on the results of several carefully designed studies and the extensive clinical experience of experts. Most of the studies have involved people with full symptoms of panic disorder, with or without agoraphobia. But there's no reason to suspect that you won't benefit from these techniques if you have less intense or less frequent panic attacks. Two main types of treatment have been evaluated:

- **Psychological interventions** – particularly techniques that fall under the broad heading of cognitive behavioural therapy.

- **Medications** – especially using groups of drugs called *the selective serotonin reuptake inhibitors* (SSRIs), the *tricyclics*, which have traditionally been used to treat depression and the *benzodiazepines*, which are sometimes called the minor tranquillizers.

The six-step self-help course in Parts Two and Three is based on a cognitive behavioural approach to managing your symptoms. This chapter gives a brief outline of relevant medications, but it's important to ask your doctor for more detailed information – in most countries only medical practitioners can prescribe these treatments. You might also be offered other types of treatment, but it's always best to talk to your doctor first about these approaches. They include:

- Traditional psychotherapy based on psychoanalytical principles

- Family and marital therapy

- Various newer psychotherapies

Medications

Experts differ in their views on using medications to treat panic disorder – but doctors most commonly prescribe SSRIs when you opt for this type of treatment. These days SSRIs have largely replaced two older families of drugs called the benzodiazepines and the tricyclics, although these medications are still prescribed on some occasions. Some therapists are concerned about relying too heavily on medications because:

- Some people don't want to take medication

- It sometimes can have upsetting side-effects

- Some people who take certain medications may become dependent on them

- The withdrawal symptoms of some types may mimic anxiety

- Some don't make you feel better immediately – there can be a delay in feeling the therapeutic effect

- Taking medication may mean that some people are less likely to practise techniques to gain control over their panic, or to make necessary changes to their life

- When you stop taking medication, there's a risk that panic symptoms may come back

These are all things to think about if you're considering medication, or if your doctor suggests this approach. But don't let these reasons put you off completely because medication can be useful in the short term – for instance when:

- Your anxiety is severe

- You're not in a state to start practising anxiety-management techniques

- It's important that you keep on functioning

- Other circumstances mean that it's difficult to use psychological treatments

It's best to try non-drug approaches wherever possible, even if you're also using medication. And you should only use medication when an experienced medical practitioner is directly supervising your treatment. This is important – your doctor will be able to discuss the treatment with you and look at whether it is appropriate for you. For instance, you may have a medical condition and be using other medicines. The doctor will also be able to monitor the dose carefully and pick up on, discuss and manage any side-effects. Also, your doctor can withdraw the medication gradually, over time.

Types of medicines

Selective serotonin re-uptake inhibitors (SSRIs)

The major guidelines suggest that if a doctor is going to prescribe medication for panic disorder, the first-line treatment should be an SSRI. It's thought that the main way in which these drugs work is by increasing the availability of a brain chemical called serotonin, at the point where it carries messages between different nerves.

SSRIs were introduced as antidepressants, but it's now accepted that they're effective for panic disorder because they can reduce anxiety and symptoms of phobia – and of course reduce any depression. You might have heard of some of the individual drugs such as fluoxetine, sertraline, fluvoxamine and paroxetine – new ones are being added to the list quite frequently. There's no water-tight evidence to show that one is better than another, so it may be a case of working with your doctor in a trial-and-error approach to find which one works best for you.

There are also related drugs such as mirtazepine and venlafaxine that work on different chemical transmitters in your brain. But more research is needed to find out whether these medications are effective for panic disorder.

Key points of SSRIs:

- SSRIs tend to be safer than the tricyclics, especially if you've got certain heart, kidney or eye problems – although you'll need a lower dose if you have liver disease. Your doctor may also prescribe a lower dose depending on your age and ethnic group.

- These drugs shouldn't be prescribed for children unless there are special circumstances.

- SSRIs can cause some side-effects, usually at the beginning of treatment, but these are not dangerous and shouldn't bother you too much. They include: headache, nausea, vomiting, gastric upset, insomnia and sexual problems.

- You may find that you're more irritable and agitated than usual when you start taking this type of medication. So it's important to start with a low dose and allow your doctor to increase it slowly.

- It can take up to four weeks or longer to feel the full anti-panic effects of these drugs – it can be a gradual build up so it's important to be patient.

Always discuss any worries with your doctor when you start a course of drug treatment – this will help you to agree on the best course of action, such as changing to a different drug, dealing with any side-effects or trying a different dose. It's important to carry on taking the medication in the way you've discussed with your doctor – for instance don't stop taking it suddenly. If you do, you may experience side-effects that mimic anxiety.

It's usually possible to come off the medication with few problems, under your doctor's supervision. But when and how you do this depends on how you've responded to the treatment, how well you've mastered psychological techniques to deal with your panic and the current stresses in your life.

Tricyclics

This group of medications was first introduced to treat depression, but since then they've been used to treat panic disorder, obsessive-compulsive disorder and chronic pain. You might have heard of one called imipramine – this, along with related tricyclic medicines such as clomipramine, can reduce symptoms of panic disorder. These drugs also seem to increase the activity of neurotransmitters such as noradrenaline and serotonin, which carry signals across nerves.

Tricyclics are effective for panic and associated depression, and in some countries they're still the first-line treatment for panic because they're cheaper than newer drugs. Your doctor might suggest this type of medication if you've found that SSRIs don't work for you, or you experience unpleasant side-effects.

Another family of drugs called monoamine oxidase inhibitors (MAOIs) were introduced around the same time as the tricyclics and used to treat anxiety – particularly 'atypical' cases where someone has a mixture of anxiety, depression and physical symptoms. Newer MAOIs have been developed since then, but doctors don't commonly prescribe these drugs for panic disorder.

Key points about tricyclics:

- You generally take these medications at night because they can have a sedative effect.

- Your doctor will gradually increase the dose, to minimize any side-effects.

- It will probably take between one and three weeks to notice any benefits.

- Side-effects include: sedation, a dry mouth, blurred vision, constipation, dizziness on standing up, tremor and sweating.

- People with panic disorder sometimes feel jittery and tense when they start to take these medications, so your doctor will usually build up the dose gradually.

- Any side-effects tend to subside after a few weeks of treatment.

- These drugs are safe for healthy people, but they may not be suitable if you have a major physical disease such as heart, kidney, bladder or certain eye problems. Your doctor may do some tests to check that this type of drug is suitable for you to use.

- Your doctor may also prescribe a lower dose depending on your age and ethnic group.

- There are health risks if you take too much, or if you take the medication with other drugs or alcohol. They should not be taken by people who are suicidal.

As with SSRIs, it's important to talk to your doctor about any side-effects or worries about your medication. And make sure that anyone close to you knows what medications you're using.

Benzodiazepines

Unlike the tricyclics and especially the SSRIs, doctors are in less agreement about when and how to prescribe benzodiazepines for panic disorder. Alprazolam, which is as effective as the tricyclic imipramine, has been studied most extensively for panic disorder. You also might have heard of some of the others in this family such as diazepam, clonazepam and lorazepam.

Key points about this type of medication:

- One advantage is that they are effective anti-anxiety drugs that work more quickly than other types of medications.

- They have side-effects – the most important are sedation and the way they interfere with your concentration. But because they can help you sleep, they may be useful in certain circumstances. These drugs can also cause slurred speech, and problems with your balance and memory.

- Because of the side-effects, it's important not to drive or operate dangerous machinery. Older people are especially at risk because of the dangers involved with having a fall or becoming confused.

- You can develop a tolerance to these medications – so over time you may be tempted to increase the dose to achieve the same effect.

- You can become dependent on benzodiazepines – and if you stop taking these medications too quickly you can experience unpleasant withdrawal-effects, so your doctor needs to monitor any reduction in the dose. If you've got a history of drug or alcohol dependence, benzodiazepines may not be a suitable treatment for you.

- The withdrawal can mimic panic symptoms, which means coming off the treatment may not be an attractive option.

- Many doctors favour using these drugs selectively and for a short period only – the aim is to substitute non-drug methods to control anxiety in the long term.

Other medications

Occasionally, doctors will prescribe a beta-blocker – this type of drug is usually used to treat high blood pressure and some other heart problems. These medications, as well as another drug called clonidine, reduce some of the physical symptoms of panic – especially tremor and rapid heartbeat. But they have little effect on the psychological symptoms that occur during a panic attack, such as catastrophic thinking. Even so, some people find that it's easier to cope with their attacks when the physical symptoms of panic are less intense.

Buspirone is another medication that has been used successfully to treat various types of anxiety, although most often this is 'generalized' anxiety rather than panic. But it might take a few weeks of treatment to achieve the maximum benefit, in a similar way to the antidepressant medications discussed earlier. Other classes of drugs, such as the mood stabilizers, valproate and carbamazepine, are also beginning to be looked at – but more research is needed to see whether they're useful for panic disorder.

Psychological treatments

CASE STUDY: Lorraine

'At first, when the attacks started, I thought they would just go away by themselves. When they lasted for a few months, I began to realize that I had to do something about them. I never considered that this would require psychological treatment. The symptoms seemed so physical, like I was having a heart attack or something, and I just wanted a fast cure. I wanted to find a way to stop the attacks immediately.'

Doctors and therapists use several types of psychological approaches to treat panic disorder. This self-help course uses techniques drawn mainly from the principles of *cognitive behavioural therapy* – our inner thought processes are known as *cognitive mechanisms*. When these approaches are applied systematically, they can have a major impact on problems such as panic and agoraphobia. And one of the real benefits is that these techniques lend themselves well to a self-help approach.

Cognitive behavioural therapy is based on the principles of *learning theory*. The idea is that many types of behaviour, and the symptoms they cause, develop as a result of a repeated pattern of responses to conditions in our environment. So we can develop 'faulty' habits in the way we respond to environmental or physical stress, and it's these learnt behaviours that can be upsetting.

CASE STUDY: David

'By the time I get off the bus, the symptoms have lessened. Why do these attacks start and stop for no reason? I feel drained, exhausted and weak. I can't think straight. Maybe I should give up taking the bus for a while. Or should I go to the hospital for another check-up? I don't know. I can't cope with this any more. All I know is that I spend most of my time worrying about having another attack. I can't go on like this or my whole life will be ruined.'

David has 'learnt' that getting on a bus makes him anxious – every time he waits at the bus stop he's frightened he'll have a panic attack on the bus. This makes him even more anxious – he's developed a 'faulty' habit. And his behaviour – panic attacks, avoiding the bus and having check-ups at the hospital – distresses him further.

If these habits can be *learnt*, then it's possible to *unlearn* them and to *relearn* better ways of coping – ways that don't cause distress and make life difficult. So cognitive behavioural therapy can help you learn new ways of dealing with difficult situations, and the anxieties that they may cause, by practice and repetition.

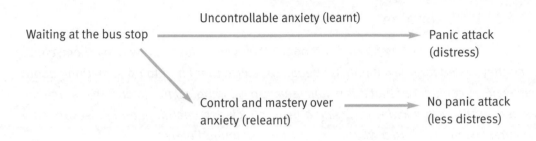

There are several types of learning. Some types can lead to unhelpful habits, which can produce symptoms of anxiety:

- **Conditioning** – for example, if you repeatedly experience panic in a supermarket, you become conditioned to feel afraid whenever you go into a supermarket, even if you're not actually being threatened.

- **Avoidance** – by steering clear of supermarkets you also avoid the unpleasant emotions associated with fear.

- **Feeling relieved** – this only serves to reinforce your desire to avoid the supermarket. It's likely that your agoraphobic symptoms will get worse and, once they're established, it can be difficult to undo avoidance.

It takes time to learn unhelpful habits, so it's no surprise that it also takes time to unlearn them and relearn helpful habits. The method of relearning has to be practised systematically over time – this type of treatment is called *graded exposure* or *systematic desensitization*.

In the diagram below, Penny, who doesn't attach anxiety to shopping at a supermarket, can move smoothly through the different stages of shopping. But Tina, who has experienced panic attacks in a supermarket, needs to approach the feared situation in a step-by-step manner, giving herself time to allow any feelings of fear and anxiety to settle before she leaves for home after each stage.

Penny	**Tina**
Standing in the supermarket car park	Standing in the supermarket car park
	↓
	Standing just inside the door of the supermarket
	↓
	Walking around the supermarket
	↓
	Picking up items from the shelves for her basket
↓	↓
Paying for her items at the till	Paying for her items at the till

This step-by-step approach, together with strategies that reduce anxiety, breaks Tina's connection between the supermarket and the fear response. Instead, she gradually begins to associate the supermarket with feeling at ease.

This transition usually takes time and practice. If it's done too quickly – say Tina tries to do it in two stages rather than five – the over-rapid exposure to her feared situation may make her anxiety worse. That's why exposure (used together with anxiety-reduction techniques) needs to be gradual, starting from the least anxiety-provoking situations to those that cause most fear. It's also important to practise this regularly as part of a systematic programme – if you practise the exercises only occasionally, it leaves time for your old habits to resurface between attempts.

Your inner thought processes (cognitive mechanisms) also play an important role in learning. The *A-B-C model* developed by Albert Ellis, a pioneer in the field of cognitive therapy, is a good way to understand this type of learning:

- **A** refers to a situation, place or event in the outside world.

- **B** is the way we interpret or think about that event and, according to cognitive theory, it's critical to human learning. Often it's not the outside event itself that makes us feel depressed or anxious, but the way we interpret that event.

- **C** is our emotional or behavioural response to the event.

It's easy to see from our own experience that the same event can affect people in very different ways. Take the example of Ben, a manager who arrives at the office clearly in an angry mood. Two of Ben's staff – Peter and Tony – react in different ways:

Ben arrives in an angry mood

Peter assumes he's done something wrong and believes he needs to work harder to please Ben.

Tony simply shrugs and assumes that something has gone wrong in Ben's private life as has happened before, and that his bad mood has nothing to do with him.

Peter becomes anxious, worried and guilty and may work longer hours

Tony continues with his normal work in the expectation that Ben's mood will improve.

You can apply cognitive techniques to help you identify, reconsider and, if necessary, alter unrealistically negative interpretations of events or situations. You can probably remember a time when you made yourself anxious by 'overpredicting' – you anticipated the worst outcome. So before you even entered the situation or place, and experienced how it really felt, your thought processes rang a warning bell to tell you that you might become stressed or anxious, or may even have a panic attack. As a result you were frightened of the situation and avoided it.

By keeping an eye on any negative thoughts that pop into your head, and systematically trying to change them, it's possible to reduce the anticipatory anxiety that can build up into a panic attack. Cognitive techniques are also a good way to challenge the typical catastrophic thoughts that go hand-in-hand with panic – you can learn to shorten an attack and reduce its impact on your emotions.

Cognitive behavioural therapy is useful because it allows you to break down the process – you can recognize and examine exactly how your symptoms are produced, and practise systematic methods to prevent or control them. And by looking at your problem from both a cognitive and a behavioural perspective, you can use a combination of techniques to overcome it.

Five principles will guide your recovery, and this set of workbooks will take you through the different stages. The aim is to:

- Understand the nature of your panic attacks or panic disorder, and the 'fear of fear' and 'fear of illness' cycles.

- Learn the skills to combat the symptoms of panic attacks and anxiety.

- Practise exercises to replace unhelpful or catastrophic thoughts with more helpful ones.

- Develop an approach for dealing with bodily symptoms that trigger anxiety and learn to evaluate the meaning of those sensations more realistically.

- Gradually face situations you've avoided in the past, in order to overcome agoraphobia.

Combination treatment

For some people, a combination of psychological techniques – especially cognitive behavioural approaches – and an appropriate drug treatment may be useful. But if you're having severe or frequent panic attacks, you might be too anxious to put any psychological techniques into practice straight away. Instead, it may be better to talk to your doctor about taking medication in the short term, to reduce your level of anxiety to a point where you can use cognitive behavioural strategies. Your doctor might then be able to reduce the dose gradually and you can use cognitive behavioural techniques as well, to help you to recover.

Will treatment help?

You might be afraid that you'll never recover from panic disorder. But the irony is that this fear in itself can hamper your recovery. If you keep in mind that most people with panic disorder can benefit from using cognitive behavioural approaches, it may help you feel more positive about trying this self-help course. Cognitive behavioural therapy is one of the most heavily researched and well-established psychological treatments for panic disorder. Other psychological treatments are available, but their long-term effectiveness is less well known.

Once you've learnt how to control and then prevent panic attacks, you can remain symptom-free for long periods – often several years. Even if you experience some symptoms at a later stage, these are usually less severe and easier to control. So it really is worthwhile to help yourself by learning how to manage your anxiety. You'll feel the benefits immediately, as well as for years to come.

Summary

- Research shows that both psychological and drug treatments can be effective for treating panic disorder, and most people make a good recovery. The two types of treatments can be used alone, or in combination.

- The selective serotonin re-uptake inhibitors (SSRIs) have become the standard medical treatment for panic disorder.

- You may not like the idea of taking a medication, and each of the different types can have side-effects. But drug treatment may be useful in certain circumstances – for instance if you are too anxious to make use of psychological treatments.

- Cognitive behaviour therapy – on which this self-help course is based – can have a major impact on panic disorder and agoraphobia.

- Unhelpful habits are learnt, which means that they can be unlearnt and replaced with helpful habits. If you expose yourself gradually to the situation or place you fear, you can desensitize yourself to whatever you fear – and, in time, reduce your anxiety. But you need to do this step by step, otherwise you could make your anxiety worse.

- Don't be afraid that you won't recover from panic disorder. Over 80 per cent of people do so by using cognitive behaviour therapy techniques, and these methods lend themselves to an effective self-help approach.

SECTION 5: The Defining Features of Panic and Agoraphobia

This section will help you understand:

- The definition of panic attacks and panic disorder

- The definition of agoraphobia

- How common panic disorder and agoraphobia are

- How these conditions are linked to other anxiety disorders

The definition of panic attacks and panic disorder

Agoraphobia has been recognized for a long time, but it wasn't until 1980 that panic disorder was added to the American psychiatric classificatory system, the *Diagnostic and Statistical Manual of Mental Disorders*, third edition *(DSM-III)*. Until then, panic disorder was seen as a type of 'anxiety neurosis', which included many different types of anxiety.

Panic attacks

For your doctor to diagnose a panic attack, the fourth and most recent edition of the *DSM (DSM-IV)* says that you have to have at least four of a list of thirteen symptoms listed below. Most people experience more than four symptoms when they have a panic attack, and you might have experienced different types of symptoms on different occasions.

Tick the boxes on the left of the checklist if you've experienced any of these symptoms before.

The defining features of panic attacks

A panic attack is an episode of intense fear or discomfort in which four (or more) of the following symptoms develop abruptly and reach a peak within ten minutes:

☐ 1 Palpitations, pounding heart or accelerated heart rate

☐ 2 Sweating

☐ 3 Trembling or shaking

☐ 4 Sensations of shortness of breath or smothering

☐ 5 Feeling of choking

☐ 6 Chest pain or discomfort

☐ 7 Nausea or abdominal distress

☐ 8 Feeling dizzy, unsteady, light-headed or faint

☐ 9 Derealization (feelings of unreality) or depersonalization (being detached from oneself)

☐ 10 Fear of losing control or going crazy

☐ 11 Fear of dying

☐ 12 Paresthesias (numbness or tingling sensations)

☐ 13 Chills or hot flushes

Source: adapted from *DSM-IV* (American Psychiatric Association, 1994).

Panic disorder

For your doctor to make a diagnosis of panic disorder, you must have regular panic attacks and have a period of at least one month in which you fear having further panic attacks.

Tick the boxes on the left of the checklist below if any of the features apply to you.

The defining features of panic disorder

Both (1) and (2) must be present:

☐ 1 Recurrent unexpected panic attacks (see the 'defining features of panic attacks' checklist, above); and

☐ 2 At least one of the attacks is followed by one month (or more) of one (or more) of the following:

☐ **(a)** persistent concern about having additional attacks;

☐ **(b)** worry about the implications of the attack or its consequences (e.g. losing control, having a heart attack, 'going crazy');

☐ **(c)** a significant change in routine or in usual activities because of the panic attacks (e.g. avoiding shopping centres).

Source: adapted from *DSM-IV* (American Psychiatric Association, 1994).

The definition of agoraphobia

The DSM classifies panic disorder as occurring with or without agoraphobia. The checklist below sets out the defining features of agoraphobia. Some people may have agoraphobia without ever having panic disorder, or they may have some other underlying disorder, such as depression, associated with agoraphobic behaviour.

Tick the boxes on the left of the checklist below if any of the features apply to you.

The defining features of agoraphobia

☐ You feel anxiety about being in places or situations from which escape might be difficult (or embarrassing) or in which help may not be available in the event of having a panic attack.

☐ You avoid the situations or else endure them but with marked distress or with anxiety about having a panic attack, or require the presence of a companion.

Source: adapted from *DSM-IV* (American Psychiatric Association, 1994).

How common are panic disorder and agoraphobia?

About 23 per cent of people experience at least one unexpected panic attack in their lifetime. Figures vary for panic disorder, but around 4 per cent of people have this condition at some time in their lives. More women than men are affected – about two-thirds of people with panic disorder are female. Around 30 per cent of people with panic disorder also develop agoraphobia.

It's common for panic disorder to begin in the mid to late twenties, but it can first affect you at any age. Many people don't seek treatment at all – those who do are usually in their mid-thirties.

Panic, agoraphobia and other anxiety disorders

Certain situations set off panic attacks for some people, but they can also be caused by other anxiety disorders:

- **Phobias** – some people develop panic symptoms when they're exposed to specific objects or situations such as spiders, heights or air travel.

- **Social phobia** – this is an intense anxiety that some people experience when they're in a situation of scrutiny, such as eating in public or having to make a speech.

- **Obsessive-compulsive disorder** – some people can become very anxious about becoming contaminated, or if they cannot complete their recurrent rituals of checking, counting or washing.

- **Post-traumatic stress disorder** – this can follow a life-threatening traumatic event, and may cause people to startle easily or become extremely anxious if they're exposed to reminders of their trauma.

- **Generalized anxiety disorder** (GAD) may be associated with panic disorder. People with GAD experience anxiety symptoms most of the time and tend to worry excessively or unnecessarily about many things. In its pure form it does not include acute attacks of panic. There's a great deal of overlap between the two conditions, but most research studies have found differences between them in terms of family history, inheritance patterns and people's responses to specific treatments.

- **Separation anxiety disorder** – children and some adults have intense fears of separation from persons close to them and they may panic when this happens.

All of these conditions belong to the 'family' of anxiety disorders – some people may have more than one, where the symptoms of each overlap. But it's worth trying to get an accurate diagnosis from your doctor to sort out which form of anxiety is most prominent. For most forms, it's likely that you'll find general stress-management techniques helpful. But it's becoming increasingly apparent that each type of anxiety disorder responds best to a specific technique, rather than a general stress-management approach. The closer the match between diagnosis and management, the better the outcome.

After you've finished working through the six-step self-help course in Parts Two and Three, you may find it useful to gather more information about treatments for general stress and anxiety symptoms. There's also a set of workbooks for stress management in this series, which you might find helpful. Alternatively, it can be a good idea to speak to your doctor to get details of other treatment programmes.

In the next part of this course, you will start the six-step self-help course and learn to recognize when you're anxious and what is triggering panic in you. You'll also learn how to recognize the factors in your lifestyle that may be contributing and how to start controlling your panic.

Summary

- Panic attacks, panic disorder and agoraphobia have specific definitions, set out by the American Psychiatric Association's classification system, the *Diagnostic and Statistical Manual of Mental Disorders*.

- Around 10 per cent of people have at least one unexpected panic attack in their lifetime, and up to 6 per cent have panic disorder at some time in their lives.

- Two-thirds of people with panic disorder are female. The condition usually appears in the mid to late twenties, but it can first affect people at any age.

- People can experience panic attacks and panic symptoms in a number of other anxiety disorders. But there are different techniques to manage each of the anxiety disorders, so it's worth seeking professional help to find the best match for your particular condition.

Extra Charts and Worksheets

Coping mechanism	Effects

Coping mechanism	Effects

Coping mechanism	Effects

Coping mechanism	Effects

62

Thoughts and Reflections

Thoughts and Reflections

64

Thoughts and Reflections

Thoughts and Reflections

Thoughts and Reflections